YOUR KNOWLEDGE HAS VALUE

- We will publish your bachelor's and master's thesis, essays and papers

- Your own eBook and book - sold worldwide in all relevant shops

- Earn money with each sale

Upload your text at www.GRIN.com
and publish for free

Bibliographic information published by the German National Library:

The German National Library lists this publication in the National Bibliography; detailed bibliographic data are available on the Internet at http://dnb.dnb.de .

This book is copyright material and must not be copied, reproduced, transferred, distributed, leased, licensed or publicly performed or used in any way except as specifically permitted in writing by the publishers, as allowed under the terms and conditions under which it was purchased or as strictly permitted by applicable copyright law. Any unauthorized distribution or use of this text may be a direct infringement of the author s and publisher s rights and those responsible may be liable in law accordingly.

Imprint:

Copyright © 2018 GRIN Verlag
Print and binding: Books on Demand GmbH, Norderstedt Germany
ISBN: 9783668732964

This book at GRIN:

https://www.grin.com/document/429851

Caroline Mutuku

Diamonds Pricing and Ethical Issues Surrounding Diamonds

GRIN Verlag

GRIN - Your knowledge has value

Since its foundation in 1998, GRIN has specialized in publishing academic texts by students, college teachers and other academics as e-book and printed book. The website www.grin.com is an ideal platform for presenting term papers, final papers, scientific essays, dissertations and specialist books.

Visit us on the internet:

http://www.grin.com/

http://www.facebook.com/grincom

http://www.twitter.com/grin_com

Diamonds Pricing and Ethical Issues Surrounding Diamonds

Table of Contents

Introduction 2
History of Diamond and Diamond Trading 2
    Return Characteristics of Diamonds 4
Current Market Structure 5
Diamonds' Characteristics 6
Ethical Issues (Diamond Conflict) 7
Valuing Diamonds 9
Conclusion 10
References 11

Introduction

Diamonds are believed to be among the most precious commodities for trade. In the past three centuries, diamond has been considered to as one of the rare mineral elements in the earth's crust. However, the immense demand for diamond by the global population appears to be the most probable reason as to why diamond has always been considered as a scarce trade commodity. Interestingly, geological findings indicate that diamonds top the list of the most abundant gem-quality colored stones. It is argued that diamond pricing is the most outstanding feature which creates unusual demand; thus, making diamonds rare (Yale University n.d.). The second reason why diamond has been considered to be scarce is the nature of its market structure. Over the years, diamond market has been characterized with an unprecedented monopoly in which a single player existed in the market. As a result, diamond pricing and its supply experienced unique market trends, and this is the principal reason as to why diamond supply chain has been manipulated to create market demand against business ethics. Yale University reports "Diamonds are rare because The De Beers Company, the world's main supplier of diamonds, makes them rare; the company controls most of the world's diamond mines and limits the quantity of diamonds supplied to the market" (p. 2). The De Beers Company has been exercising monopoly since its establishment in 1880s when Cecil Rhodes started diamond trading (Erlich & Hausel 2002). Despite the legal barriers including the U.S anti-trust laws, this company has always exercised monopoly in diamond trading. However, monopoly in the diamond market seems to end soon because its supply will increase significantly after Russia joins the market. Recently, a huge diamond field was discovered in Siberia which can supply the world market with trillion of carats in the next thirty centuries (Worstall 2012, par. 2). As a result, the structure of the diamond market is believed to change drastically in the future. Therefore, this research paper will provide an overview of diamond trading, especially with regard to the principal elements of diamond pricing.

History of Diamond and Diamond Trading

Historically, diamonds are known as beautiful objects of desire and their history is quite long. This is probably the principal reason as to why Pliny, a Roman naturalist remarked "diamond is the most valuable, not only of precious stones, but of all things in this world" (Gemological Institute of America 2014, par. 1). Precisely, the history of diamonds reflects the beauty and mystical powers combined with commercial expertise.

Despite the old-age myths, which overshadowed the history of diamonds including the mythical valley of diamonds which was said to have been guarded by venomous snakes, the magnificent nature of diamonds history unearth some of the most remarkable moments in the development of ancient cultures. According to the early history, diamonds date as early as thirty centuries. Gemological Institute of America (2014, par. 3) reports "the world's love of diamonds had its start in India, where diamonds were gathered from the country's rivers and streams. Some historians estimate that India was trading in diamonds as early as the fourth century BC". It is believed that, diamonds became valued for its ability to refract light. In those days, Indians used diamonds for decorative purposes in their works of art. It is also believed that, diamonds were used as a talisman. As such, they provided protection in battles, as well as, warding of evil.

It is believed that, intensive exploitation of diamonds in India for commercial purposes led to the depletion of diamond mines in the early 1700s. This disruption of diamond supply from India led to an intensive search for the commodity in other parts of the world. Thereafter, Brazil became one of the earliest sources of diamond where diamond was discovered by gold miners along river banks. Historians believe that the extensive demand for diamond enabled Brazil to exercise dominance in the diamond market for one and half centuries. Unfortunately, diamond trading declined drastically in the late 1700s owing to the impact of the French Revolution which influenced wealth distribution among the most potential diamond consumers who served as the ruling classes. This was so because; Brazil relied on the European market for its diamond; thus, political upheavals in Western Europe disrupted diamond supply, leading to devastating economic consequences on Brazil's diamond (Gemological Institute of America 2014).

However, diamond market was greeted with an unprecedented demand at the beginning of the 1800s. For instance, the United States and Western Europe gained significant affluence after European explorers discovered vast treasures of diamond in South Africa leading to the broadening of the diamond trade.

The discovery of diamond deposits in Kimberley, South Africa in 1866 marked the beginning of the modern diamond trading history. Later on in 1888, Cecil Rhodes, a British Businessman established the De Beers Company to control diamond mines in South Africa. It is reported that, De Beers Company gained control of the diamond market by 1900 in which it held 90% of the world's diamond supply. However, it is worth noting that diamond market faced enormous challenges, especially in mining because surface diamond became depleted. As a result, underground diamond proved highly costly, and this caused a significant decline of diamond production. It is believed that, these challenges in diamond mining prompted miners to adopt efficient mining techniques in the effort of reducing the cost of production. In addition, diamond cutting and polishing emerged as some of the most cost reducing techniques, although these techniques improved the "appearance of finished stones" (Gemological Institute of America 2014, par. 8).

In the 1920s, diamond production had increased significantly to reach 3 million carats from the low production of less than a million carats, in 1870s. Thereafter, diamond production increased immensely to reach 50 million carats by 1970s, and this production doubled by 1990s in which the annual diamond production was 100 million carats. This was relatively low compared to the current yearly production in which 125.6 million carats produced in 2011 (Israel Diamond Institute 2012).

In regard to rough diamond supply, African continent served as the leading diamond producer by the end of 1970s although Soviet Union produced a significant share in the diamond market. It is believed that, South Africa and Soviet Union supplied the diamond market with high-quality diamond in 1980s, whereas Zaire produced low-quality diamond. However, the discovery of a new diamond mine in Botswana, in 1982 increased production of high-quality diamond to enable the country to attain the third rank for diamond recovery in the world. This discovery prompted the De Beers Company to persuade the government of Botswana, in order to gain control of diamond mining in the South African region. As a result, Botswana established a diamond-cutting industry through a contract with De Beers Company. Thereafter, diamond market experienced an immense expansion after diamond was discovered in other parts of the world including Australia and Canada, although diamond trading did not attract significant scientific research until recently (Gemological Institute of America 2014).

Return Characteristics of Diamonds

It has been found out that the return characteristics of diamonds are quite different from those of other precious stones in the market. These changes are attributable to the ethical considerations which surround diamonds trading. Another significant factor which determines the return characteristics of diamonds is the history of diamonds investment which reflects elements of monopoly in an imperfect market which allows unscrupulous dealers to hoard the commodity for the purpose of creating inadequacy in diamond supplies in the market. This aspect is also influenced by the current market structure of diamonds trading, although it seems to have changed from monopoly to oligopoly structure after many players in diamonds trading joined the global diamonds market. However, diamond valuing remain to be a significant factor that influences the return characteristics of diamonds, especially in regard to the metrics used in diamonds pricing.

In general, diamonds trading has been found to be associated with low CAMP. It also bears low correlations with gold, long-term US bond prices and the S&P 500. Moreover, diamonds trading has been found to exhibit low correlations with the US inflation. In comparison with gold, diamond investment involves enormous risks because it does not withstand extreme shocks on the stock market, whereas gold can be synchronized with stocks. Schiemenz (2012, p. 25) states "gold can be regarded as a safe haven investment in the context of extreme shocks occurring on stock markets on a daily basis…, in conditions of extreme market uncertainty, gold moves synchronous with stocks and other risky assets." Evidence for diamonds correlation can be provided by the three different economic phases in the U.S economy: expansion 2002-2006, recession 2007-2009 and recovery 2010-2013. Diamond trading proved to be a risky investment because is not responding to stock market changes in a synchronized manner as it was the case with gold. As such, it is believed to contribute to the US inflation. However, it is worth noting that diamonds returns are influenced by the number of wealthy investors in high valued diamonds. It is believed that the increase of wealthy investors has led to the soaring prices (Kolesnikov-Jessop 2013). In regard to the liquidity of the diamond market, diamond trading is correlated to low liquidity costs, and this influences diamond pricing. This has been so because; investors experience challenges in buying and selling of diamonds in the secondary markets, although the proposed move of introducing exchange-traded fund is expected to ease trading.

Current Market Structure

Diamond market structure has always been characterized with monopoly in which De Beers Company controls diamond marketing in the world. Yale University (n.d., p. 2) reports that since 1889, "large diamond deposits have been discovered in other African countries, Russia, Australia, and India. De Beers has either bought out new producers or entered into agreements with local governments." This implies that De Beers controls diamond marketing in the world, and this is the reason as to why it has been exercising monopoly in the global diamond market. This aspect is reaffirmed by Zimnisky (2013, par. 1) who states "De Beers was the diamond industry, and diamonds were synonymous with De Beers."

It is argued that the structure of the diamond market encompassed structural flaws owing the impact of monopoly exercised by De Beers, a single player in the diamond market. De Beers had been controlling diamond market since its establishment in 1880s. Cecil Rhodes is believed to have bought many diamond mines in different countries through contracting its marketing during the 1800s diamond rush, in which the company controlled diamond supply in the world. However, new players emerged in the early 20th century and challenged De Beers' monopoly. One of these new players was Ernest Oppenheimer who bought shares from De Beers and gained control of the company by 1920s. In response to Ernest Oppenheimer's influence in the diamond market, De Beers sought to influence diamond producers to market it through De Beers Company. As a result, De Beers extended its dominance over diamond supply in the global diamond market because it was able to control diamond supply from non-De Beers mines in various parts of the world. This approach enabled De Beers to maintain its monopoly in the diamond market through its new channel known as the Central Selling Organization (CSO). Later on, the Central Selling Organization changed its name to Diamond Trading Co (DTC) through which De Beers stockpiled inventory in the diamond's weak market because membership as a 'sight-holder' prevented the establishment of a free-market structure. It is believed that drastic changes in the diamond market have changed its structure in the past 25 years. It has changed from a monopoly structure which was controlled by the De Beers Company for 100 years to a free market which is driven by market forces (Zimnisky 2013).

However, the current market structure operates in secondary market basis in which retailers "buy inventory from a trusted wholesaler or they can buy from a customer at a discount to wholesale, but take on greater risk of what they are buying in the process" (Zimnisky 2014, par. 31).

Diamonds' Characteristics

Diamonds bear a range of characteristics. One of the most outstanding characteristics of diamond is that it is the hardest metal element on Earth. This is the principal reason as to why rough diamond is used in making cutting tools such as drilling devices. It is believed that diamond's hardness develops during its formation in the earth's crust. The second characteristic of diamond is its heat conductivity in which diamond is known to conduct heat faster than other metals. It has been found out "diamond conducts heat 5 times faster than copper, which is why it feels cold to the touch" (Natural History Museum n.d., par. 2).

Another significant characteristic of diamond is that, it is transparent in nature. Therefore, pure diamond can be identified from its transparent appearance because it is believed to be the most transparent metal element in the world. As such, diamond reflects light: ultra-violet light, visible light and infrared light, and this is probably the principal reason as to why Indians and Greeks used diamond for aesthetic purposes. It is also believed that diamond can survive the corrosive effect of chemicals in the environment including radioactive substance for a long duration. Moreover, diamond bears unique electrical conductivity properties because it can be used both as a conductor or an insulator (Natural History Museum n.d.). Another unique characteristic with diamond is that, it does not trigger an immune response when ingested into the human body as it is the case with most metals, and this explains why diamond miners smuggled diamond out of the mines through ingesting it in the Middle Age.

Ethical Issues (Diamond Conflict)

Despite the flourishing of the diamond market, ethical issues are currently emerging which compromise the process of diamond trading. One of the most challenging ethical issues associated with diamond trading is the conflict issue, which has led to violence and tyranny in some areas where diamond is mined. Recently, Global Witness, an international environmental group explained several issues related diamond mining. In theory, diamond trading in conflict regions have become known to as 'conflict diamonds' because they are believed to fuel conflict (Bourne & Reimann 2001). However, it is worth noting that the issue of 'conflict diamonds' or the so-called 'blood diamonds' encompasses immense controversy. In practice, it is argued that the Kimberley process has created opportunities for diamond cartels to use revenues from diamond trading for financing armed conflict. Armstrong (2011, par. 1) reports "A major international environmental group has pulled out of the process to guarantee that diamonds do not come from conflict zones, saying the Kimberley Process had refused to evolve and address the clear links between diamonds, violence and tyranny."

In this light, it is worth evaluating the Kimberley Process which is claimed to facilitate conflict in diamond mining regions, and identify the so-called 'conflict diamonds'. It is also worth noting the population which is affected by the issue of 'conflict diamonds'. Ideally, 'conflict diamonds' have been found to be traded illegally to generate funds for financing conflict in some of the war-torn African countries, especially in western and central Africa (Bourne & Reimann 2001). This information has been obtained by the World

Diamond Council whose mandate is to represent the commercial diamond trade in the global market. According to Armstrong (2011, par. 3) United Nations defines 'conflict diamonds' as "diamonds that originate from areas controlled by forces or factions opposed to legitimate and internationally recognized governments, and are used to fund military action in opposition to those governments, or in contravention of the decisions of the Security Council." Further information reveals that, 'conflict diamonds' are "generally in 'rough' form, meaning they have recently been extracted and not yet cut" (Armstrong 2011, par. 4). One of the most outstanding examples of conflicts funded with revenue from 'conflict diamonds' is the perennial civil war in Sierra Leone, which is said to have consumed 4% of the world's diamond production (Armstrong 2011).

In the past two decades, the Diamond Market Council has been looking for the most appropriate ways of eliminating illegal trade of 'conflict diamonds' and one of these approaches was the Kimberley Process. Kimberley Process was formed by Southern African countries which produce diamond, in May 2000 in the effort of putting into a halt diamond purchases related to violence funding. In this convention whose principal stakeholders were the UN, the governments of 74 countries, EU, Global Witness and the World Diamond Council, the so-called the Kimberley Process Certification Scheme (KPCS) was signed to ensure that legitimate trading of rough diamond exports (Armstrong 2011).

However, it is emerging that the Kimberley Process has not addressed the issue of 'conflict diamonds'. It is argued that, the failure of the Kimberley Process to prevent illegal trading of diamond has caused immense suffering in some areas. Despite the suffering experienced by people who are caught in the conflict, it is emerging that thousands of people are held as slaves in diamond mines to extract rough diamond. This incident was reported in Sierra Leone during the civil war in which captives were forced to dig gravel with their bare hands. Elsewhere, in the Democratic Republic of Congo, rebel fighters are said to have hijacked diamond trade in mineral ores and subjected "the local population to massacres, rape, extortion, and forced labor" (Armstrong 2011, par. 15).'Conflict diamonds' have also been used to fund conflict in Angola. Surprisingly, 'conflict diamonds' are being used to fund terrorist activities by Al-Qaeda (Global Witness 2014). Therefore, it is evident that diamond trading is associated with numerous ethical issues.

Valuing Diamonds

In regard to the valuing of diamond, diamonds are valued depending on various parameters. Ordinarily, diamonds are valued based on diamond cutting, color, carat weight and clarity. Precisely, these features, which are considered in the pricing of diamond, are regarded to as the 4C's because they measure the quality of diamonds. In reality, carat determines the size of diamond, although diamonds' cut is believed to be the only feature of diamond, which influences diamonds' pricing because the other four features: color, clarity and carat weight are determined by the nature. In other words, these features serve as the principal parameters which are used in identifying different types of diamonds. In regard to carats, diamonds' weight is measured in the form of carats. The history of carats is rooted into the carob tree seed which was used in the early days to determine the weight of diamonds. In those days, one seed of the Carob tree was equivalent to one carat of diamond, and this was regarded to as a standard measure of diamond until recently when carats started to be expressed in terms of grams. In practice, one carat of diamond is equivalent to 0.2 grams. However, a carat is sub-divided into 100 points to ensure the accuracy in weighing diamonds. Different portions of a carat are given different pricing, although diamonds have always been priced per carat. Ideally, diamonds' carat is usually indicative of its size. However, carats are not used to determine the quality of diamonds. Instead, other features such as color, cut and clarity are used, and they also influence diamonds' pricing.

Ordinarily, uncut diamond is defined as 'rough diamond'. In its natural state, rough diamond resembles a glass pebble, and this is probably the reason as to why most people do not notice it. In reality, diamonds' brilliance serves as the most striking feature of diamonds' quality. Diamonds' brilliance is usually used as the guide for cutting the stone into facets regardless of its shape. Therefore, a well cut diamond is given a high price compared to a poorly cut one which attracts a low price. However, it is worth noting that the shape of diamonds is not used as a criterion for pricing because they do not determine the quality of diamonds. For instance, diamonds can bear different shapes, but they can be priced equally when the cuts are the same, and most diamonds in the market are cut with 58 facets (Costellos n.d.).

On the other hand, clarity is used in pricing diamonds. The aspect of clarity is determined by the presence of non-diamond crystals in the diamond which are introduced during its formation. Ordinarily, non-diamond crystals or non-crystallized carbon particles are referred to as inclusions. These inclusions are different in diamond stones, so they create unique characteristics between different pieces of diamond. In addition, these inclusions influence light passage through diamond. Therefore, a piece of diamond with little inclusions allows much light to pass, whereas a piece with many inclusions appears opaque. In diamond pricing, diamonds with few inclusions are given high prices compared to those with many inclusions. In other words, diamonds' clarity determines there values (Costellos n.d.). Ordinarily, diamond's pricing ranges from FL (flawless) to I3 (imperfect 3).

Moreover, diamonds are valued in respect to their colors. Pure diamond is absolutely colorless; thus, grading ranges from white to pink. It is believed that, diamonds whose color is closer to the white color are more valuable and rare than those with tinted colors. In general, there are yellow, blue, green, brown and pink diamonds, and each one of these has a characteristic value (Costellos n.d.).

Conclusion

In a brief conclusion, diamond investment has become one of the most profitable ventures in the world. Historically, diamond use dates back to 3000 years ago and India is believed to have established the first diamond industry. Initially, diamonds were used for aesthetic purposes, although its use for medical aid gained popularity during the Dark Ages. However, this was attributable to myths which placed significance on diamonds as healing agents. Later on, diamonds became valuable trade commodities, especially the Venice market. In the 1800s, diamond deposits were discovered in South Africa and this led to the establishment of the De Beers Company which controlled diamond marketing for over 100 years through monopolist market structure. This company influenced diamonds' pricing by controlling its supply, although diamonds' cutting, clarity, color and the carat weight serves as the principal parameters for diamonds' pricing. Currently, diamonds' market structure has changed from monopolist to oligopoly or free-market trade in which different suppliers of diamonds have joined the market and dismantled the dominance of De Beers. However, it is worth noting that, diamond trading has led to the emergence of ethical issues, especially with regard to armed conflict and terrorism in different parts of the world where diamond is mined.

References

Armstrong, P 2011, *What are 'conflict diamonds?* viewed 19 February 2018, http://edition.cnn.com/2011/12/05/world/africa/conflict-diamonds-explainer/

Bourne, M & Reimann, C 2001, *Conflict diamonds: roles, responsibilities and responses*, Bradford, UK: Department of Peace Studies, University of Bradford.

Constellos, n.d., *Valuing diamonds*, viewed 19 February 2018, http://www.costellos.com.au/diamonds/valuing.html

Erlich, E & Hausel, W 2002, *Diamond deposits: origin, exploration, and history of discovery*, Englewood, CO: SME Publishing.

Gemological Institute of America, 2014, *Diamond History and Lore*, viewed 18 February 2014, http://www.gia.edu/diamond-history-lore

Global Witness, 2014, *Conflict diamonds*, viewed 20 February 2018, http://www.globalwitness.org/campaigns/conflict/conflict-diamonds

Israel Diamond Institute, 2012, *Report: global diamond production increases in 2012*, viewed 2 February 2018, http://www.israelidiamond.co.il/english/NEWS.aspx?boneID=918&objID=11714&SearchS=annual+diamond+world+production

Kolesnikov-Jessop, S 2013, *A rising appetite to invest in colored diamonds*, viewed 27 February 2018, < http://www.nytimes.com/2013/11/18/business/international/a-rising-appetite-to-invest-in-colored-diamonds.html?_r=0>

Natural History Museum, n.d., *Properties of diamonds*, viewed 20 February 2018, http://www.nhm.ac.uk/print-version/?p=/nature-online/earth/rock-minerals/diamonds/diamond-properties/index.html

Schiemenz, E 2012, *Determinants of Gold Returns*, Berlin, Germany: epubli.

Worstall, T 2012, *Is the diamond market about to collapse over huge Russian find?*, viewed 18 February 2018, http://www.forbes.com/sites/timworstall/2012/09/18/is-the-diamond-market-about-to-collapse-over-huge-russian-find/

Yale University, n.d., *Monopoly*, viewed 19 February 2018, <http://www.econ.yale.edu/~gjh9/econ115b/slides11_4perpage.pdf>

Zimnisky, P 2013, *Diamonds: Driven by market forces for the first time in 100 years*, viewed 19 February 2018, <http://www.resourceinvestor.com/2013/04/09/diamonds-driven-by-market-forces-for-the-first-tim>

Zimnisky, P 2014, *Diamond investing FAQ*, viewed 28 February 2018, < http://www.mining.com/diamond-investing-faq-40055/>

YOUR KNOWLEDGE HAS VALUE

- We will publish your bachelor's and master's thesis, essays and papers

- Your own eBook and book -
  sold worldwide in all relevant shops

- Earn money with each sale

Upload your text at www.GRIN.com
and publish for free